A Western Activity Book

by Joanne Barkan

Table of Contents

Introduction

In the 1820s and 1830s, a few fur trappers roamed the Rocky Mountains. Some gold miners made claims in the territory that would become Colorado and Nevada. In the 1840s and 1850s, **pioneers** began to

a U.S. Army agent for the western territories

trek west across the country's plains, mountains, and deserts. Most of them didn't **settle** down until they reached California or Oregon. Thousands of **prospectors** swarmed into California in 1849. That was the year gold was discovered there, and folks couldn't get west fast enough!

Before 1860, Native Americans were the only people of any number who lived in the huge region between the Missouri River and the Sierra Nevada mountains. They had lived there for centuries. Then in the early 1860s, more and more settlers began pouring into that region. The area was known at the time as the "New West."

What did this region have to offer? Land, and lots of it!

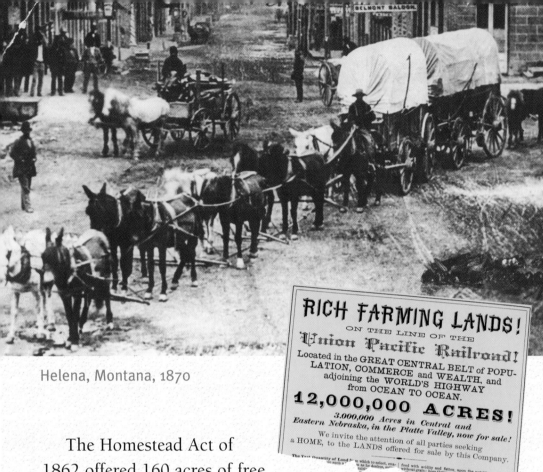

Helena, Montana, 1870

RICH FARMING LANDS!
ON THE LINE OF THE
Union Pacific Railroad!
Located in the GREAT CENTRAL BELT of POPU-
LATION, COMMERCE and WEALTH, and
adjoining the WORLD'S HIGHWAY
from OCEAN TO OCEAN.
12,000,000 ACRES!
3,000,000 Acres in Central and
Eastern Nebraska, in the Platte Valley, now for sale!
We invite the attention of all parties seeking
a HOME, to the LANDS offered for sale by this Company.

a poster advertising
railroad company land

The Homestead Act of 1862 offered 160 acres of free land in the West to any men, widows, and single women who wanted it.

The first **transcontinental** railroad was completed in 1869. Soon, six other railroad lines in the West linked up with the transcontinental. The U.S. government gave the railroad companies land for every mile of track laid, which they now offered for sale. People from eastern Europe, Canada, and Mexico bought railroad land.

Thousands of people were ready to try their luck as farmers in the West. Cattle ranchers added to the boom as they moved their herds north from Texas and settled near the railroad lines in the West.

Settlements grew into small towns and small towns grew into even larger ones. Wichita, Kansas, got started as a cattle-shipping town. Reno, Nevada, grew up where two railroad lines met. Virginia City, Nevada, was founded as a mining camp in 1859. By 1876, that little mining camp had become a bustling town of more than 23,000 people. Native Americans paid a high price for the settling of the West by outsiders. As newcomers made homes in the West, the Native Americans lost theirs. The U.S. government promised to protect Native American lands, but, time after time, it went back on its promises. The government forced the Native American nations onto **reservations**. These were areas of land set aside for Native Americans to live on.

a main street in Cheyenne, Wyoming, 1869

panning for gold in
South Dakota, 1889

This book will give you directions to do several western activities. You will

• Produce a western town newspaper

• Make and play a Native American game

• Write a cowboy song

• Cook (and eat!) a delicious western recipe

• Create a board game about life in the West

So have some fun with your classmates as you do the activities. Then double your fun by sharing these activities with your friends and family.

READ
More About It

Use library and Internet resources to read more about the West from 1862 to 1890.

A Western Newspaper

Many western towns grew with amazing speed. Businesses opened to fill every need of "boom towns" like Virginia City. Along the main street was everything from a bank to a barbershop to a **blacksmith** shop. Blacksmiths melted iron and shaped it into nails, horseshoes, and other items.

Frequently, one of the first businesses to appear was a newspaper office.

Newspapers provided much-needed information and amusement. Did the railroad raise ticket prices? Is there a square dance this week? Did a dishonest lawyer skip town?

Articles, advertisements, train schedules, and more— the newspaper told it all. Now it's your turn to make a western newspaper.

an early newspaper carrier

Ads like this might have been printed in newspapers.

Write a News Article

A news article reports a recent event. It usually answers these questions about the event: Who? What? Where? When? Why? How? The answers to these questions go in the first paragraph of the article. This is called the "lead." The less important information comes in the following paragraphs—the body of the article. The writer provides just the facts, not his or her opinions. The article might also include statements from people involved in the events.

YOUR GOAL:
Write a news article for a western town newspaper.

WHAT YOU'LL NEED:
- books and articles about life in the West between 1862 and 1890
- samples of news articles from newspapers (if possible, from western newspapers of the period)

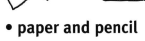

- paper and pencil
- pen or marker
- computer and printer (optional)

TIME NEEDED:
2–3 hours

What to Do:

RESEARCH THE SUBJECT

1. Read about life in a western town between 1862 and 1890.

2. Read some sample news articles. Note the **headlines**, or titles, of the articles. Note the byline—the writer's name below the headline. Note that each article starts by telling where and when it was written.

3. Make up a topic for a news article in an imaginary town's newspaper. It can be funny or serious.

4. Choose a year when your article could have appeared in a newspaper. Be sure that all the facts make sense for that year.

✓Point

Think About It

A newspaper is one thing that ties people together and helps them feel that they are part of a community. How does a newspaper do this? Why is it important? Can you think of other things or activities that serve the same purpose?

WRITE THE ARTICLE

1 Use a pencil or a computer to write a **draft** of the news article. It should be at least 100 words long. Include the city and date at the beginning of the article. If you use a computer, see if you can set the article in narrow **columns**. Don't worry about getting everything perfect. You'll have time to do that later.

2 Write a catchy headline for the article. Write your byline under the headline. Make the letter size for the headline much larger than the letter size used in the byline and the article.

3 Read your draft. Did you stick to the topic? Does the order of the information make sense? Did you add enough details? Now is the time to **revise**, or make changes to your article. When you are finished revising your article, make a clean copy.

4 Finally, **proofread** your article. Check all your spelling, grammar, and punctuation.

5 Use a pen or marker to copy your corrected article onto a new sheet of paper. If you are using a computer, print your finished article.

Make Your Newspaper

YOUR GOAL:
Assemble a western town newspaper.

WHAT YOU'LL NEED:
- your news article
- sheet of paper large enough for your article and your ad
- glue stick, paste, or rubber cement
- black pen or marker
- computer and printer (optional)

TIME NEEDED:
1 hour

What to Do:

1. Choose a name for your newspaper. Print it in large letters at the top of the sheet of paper. This is called your newspaper's logo. If you are using a computer, type and print out the logo. Then paste it onto the top of the sheet of paper.

2. You can create an ad for your newspaper if you'd like. Then arrange your news article and ad on the sheet of paper. Try different **layouts**.

3 When you have a layout that you like, paste down the article and ad, if you have made one. Share your newspaper with your family and classmates. If your teacher sets up a classroom display about the West, your newspaper will make a great addition.

THE TUMBLEWEED TIMES

vol.25 | 20 June, 1877

"LITTLE SURE SHOT" IS SCHEDULED TO APPEAR AT THIS YEAR'S COUNTY FAIR

by Hans Simon Johansson

JUNCTION CITY, KANSAS June 18, 1877
Annie Oakley and Frank Butler will be at the Davis County Fair next week to entertain folks with their sharpshooting skills. Their awesome act can be seen on Thursday afternoon on the Main Stage, right after the Ladies' Guild Pie-Cooking Contest. Another show will be Friday evening before the livestock winners are announced. (A full schedule of fair events will be printed in this Sunday's newspaper. You can also ask the following folks: Lothrop Rude, butcher; Edward Gaylord, livery stable; James C. McCoy, chemist.)

Next week's display will be Mrs. Oakley's and Mr. Butler's first show in this county since their wedding last year. Sources from up the Smoky Hill River report that the thrill-seeking couple has added some new tricks to their show. In one stunt, Oakley shoots a dime out of her husband's hand! Mrs. Oakley comes from Darke County, Ohio. She learned how to handle a gun at the tender age of eight. She earned a living shooting game before she beat famed professional sharpshooter Butler in a contest two years ago. After they got married, they began touring together. Many in town can't wait for the promised excitement.

According to local farmer Louis Brumbaugh, "I hear Annie Oakley can shoot a playing card thrown into the air 90 feet away!" Added Mrs. Elmira Brumbaugh, his wife, "We haven't had a real celebrity in this town since that Russian Grand Duke stopped by back in '72."

Visitors to the County Fair are expected to arrive as early as Friday. They will be coming from as far as Kansas City, Missouri, and Denver, Colorado Territory. The Kansas Pacific Railroad (a division of the Union Pacific Southern Branch Company) plans to add several passenger cars to its regular trains so everyone can get here. In addition to lodging at the Pacific House and Bartell Hotels, local farmers have agreed to lodge guests in their barns and haysheds.

A NATIVE AMERICAN GAME

Did you know that Native American children in the West played a game like badminton? In the badminton game we play today, we use rackets to hit a shuttlecock. A shuttlecock is a hollow cone topped with feathers. Often, modern shuttlecocks are made completely of plastic, even the "feathers."

Native Americans used wooden paddles or the palms of their hands instead of rackets. They made their shuttlecocks out of feathers attached to twigs or folded cornhusks, the leaves around ears of corn. You will make a shuttlecock with feathers. A cork stopper will take the place of twigs or cornhusks.

Native Americans also played a game like lacrosse. Here, a group of Lakota are playing the game.

Make and Play a Native American Game

YOUR GOAL:

Make a feather and cork shuttlecock and play a Native American game.

WHAT YOU'LL NEED:

- cork stopper, $1\frac{1}{4}$ to $1\frac{3}{4}$ inches long. Most hardware stores sell corks in various sizes.
- three feathers, each about 4 inches long. The quill ends should be fairly stiff. You can find feathers in craft stores.
- craft glue
- one long, thin nail
- adult helper

TIME NEEDED:

$\frac{1}{2}$ hour

What to Do:

MAKE A SHUTTLECOCK

1 Ask the adult to help you use the nail to make three holes in the cork stopper. The holes should be equally spaced on the larger flat end of the cork and about $\frac{1}{4}$ inch from the edge. Hold the nail so that the holes will angle in slightly toward the middle of the cork. Make the holes about $\frac{1}{2}$ inch deep.

2 Dab a small amount of glue on the quill end of each feather.

3 Insert the quill end of one feather into each hole in the cork.

4 Put a dab of glue where each of the three feathers enters the cork. Put the cork aside to dry.

PLAY THE SHUTTLECOCK GAME

The object of the game is to see how many times you can bat the shuttlecock into the air with the palm of your hand without letting it fall to the ground.

There are a few different ways to play:

1 If you are playing alone, see if you can bat the shuttlecock into the air five or ten times (or more!) without letting it fall to the ground.

2 If you are playing with friends, take turns batting the shuttlecock into the air. When the shuttlecock falls to the ground, the next player takes his or her turn. The player with the greatest number of "hits" wins the game.

3 You can play with a large group. Stand in a circle with the players at least six feet apart from one another. Each player bats the shuttlecock to the person standing to the right. Anyone who misses has to drop out of the circle. The winner is the last person to remain.

Cowhand Songs

From the mid-1860s to the mid-1880s, huge herds of cattle roamed the Great Plains and grazed on the western grasslands. The ranchers, who owned the cattle, hired cowhands on horseback.

The life of a cowboy in the West looks exciting in movies and TV. But to real cowhands it was probably a hard, dangerous, and sometimes lonely job. The cowboy drove the herds to wherever the grass was best. During guard duty at night, cowboys sang soft, slow songs. Sometimes they whistled or hummed.

Like most songs, cowboy songs have a number of **verses** and a **chorus** that repeats. Here are two verses and the chorus of a cowboy song you might already know.

✓ Point

Picture It

Close your eyes and picture a cowboy on horseback, singing to the herd. Then draw what you see.

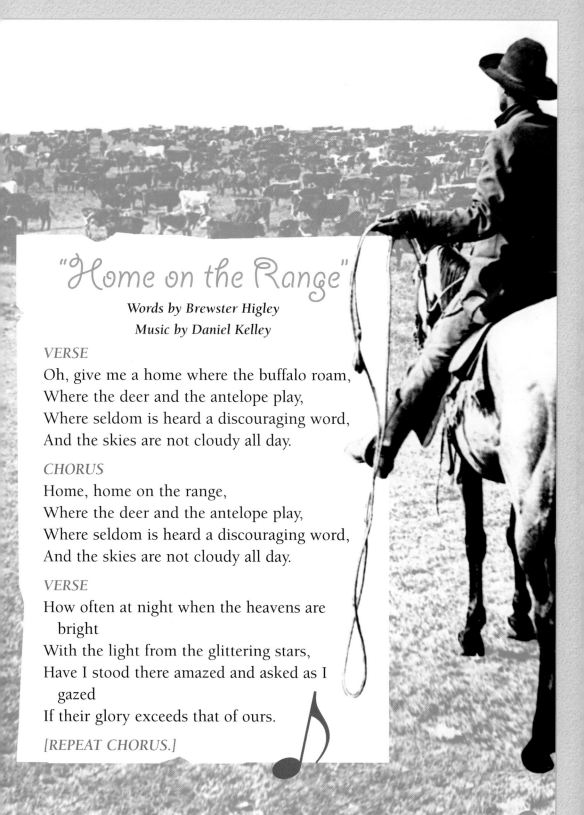

"Home on the Range"

Words by Brewster Higley
Music by Daniel Kelley

VERSE

Oh, give me a home where the buffalo roam,
Where the deer and the antelope play,
Where seldom is heard a discouraging word,
And the skies are not cloudy all day.

CHORUS

Home, home on the range,
Where the deer and the antelope play,
Where seldom is heard a discouraging word,
And the skies are not cloudy all day.

VERSE

How often at night when the heavens are
    bright
With the light from the glittering stars,
Have I stood there amazed and asked as I
    gazed
If their glory exceeds that of ours.

[REPEAT CHORUS.]

Write a Cowboy Song

YOUR GOAL:

Write a new verse for a cowboy song that you like.

WHAT YOU'LL NEED:

- **the lyrics (words) and, if possible, tunes for five or more traditional cowboy songs. You can ask the librarians at your school media center or local library for help.**
- **paper and pencil**
- **pen**
- **computer and printer (optional)**
- **musical instrument (optional)**
- **tape recorder (optional)**

TIME NEEDED:

2–3 hours

What to Do:

1 Read or listen to the cowboy songs. Select the song that you like best.

2 Write a new verse for this song. Match the number of syllables in each line and the number of lines in each verse to those in the other lines and verses.

3 Sing or say your lines out loud to see if they match the other lines in the song. Revise your verse until it is just right.

4 Proofread your verse. Then write a clean copy of the song lyrics with a pen, or print them if you're working on the computer.

5 If you know the song's tune, you can sing it. Play along on your instrument, if you have one. Ask friends and family to join in and record the song. If you don't know the tune, read the song aloud, like a poem.

It's a FACT

Cowboy poets wrote the words for many cowboy songs and then put the words to traditional tunes. Some of today's cowboys still write poetry. They meet every year at the National Cowboy Poetry Gathering.

A Pioneer Recipe

Settlers in the West had to produce many of the **ingredients**, or items of food, they used in their recipes. They raised cows, pigs, and sheep for meat. They made butter and cheese from the milk of the cows. Settlers had small gardens near their houses where they grew potatoes and other vegetables.

Cookbooks written by settler women still exist, but they don't provide detailed instructions. The cookbook writers assumed their readers would know what to do! Even if the cookbooks had good instructions, you might find some of the recipes unappealing. How does calf's head soup made with a whole calf's head sound to you?

One western recipe you would enjoy is spoonbread. It's easy and delicious!

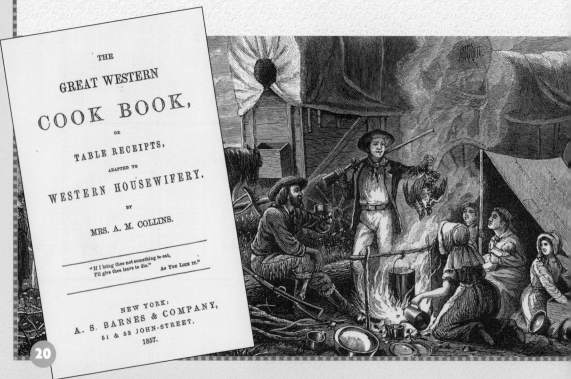

THE
GREAT WESTERN
COOK BOOK,
OR
TABLE RECEIPTS,
ADAPTED TO
WESTERN HOUSEWIFERY.
BY
MRS. A. M. COLLINS.

"If I bring thee not something to eat,
I'll give thee leave to die."   AS YOU LIKE IT."

NEW YORK:
A. S. BARNES & COMPANY,
51 & 53 JOHN-STREET,
1857.

When you follow the directions for making spoonbread, make sure you work with an adult. Use a potholder for hot dishes and pans. And don't forget to turn off the stove when you're finished.

Make Spoon Bread

YOUR GOAL:
Make a pan of spoon bread.

WHAT YOU'LL NEED:
- 1 tablespoon soft butter
- 2 tablespoons butter, divided into small bits
- 2 cups milk
- 1 cup white cornmeal
- 1 1/2 teaspoons double-acting baking power
- 1 teaspoon salt
- 3 eggs, well beaten
- pastry brush
- large wooden spoon
- 1-quart baking dish
- 1 1/2–2 quart saucepan
- oven, preheated to 375°

TIME NEEDED:
1 1/4 hours

What to Do:

1 Use the pastry brush to spread the soft butter over the bottom and sides of the baking dish. Put the dish aside.

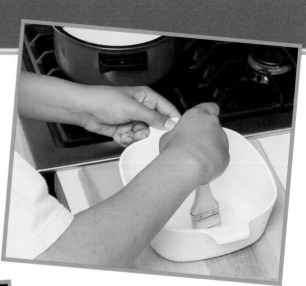

2 Pour the milk into the saucepan. Heat the milk on the stove over medium heat until you see tiny bubbles forming at the edges of the pan.

3 Pour the cornmeal slowly into the milk while stirring the mixture constantly with the wooden spoon. Don't let any lumps form.

4 Take the pan off the stove. Be sure to use potholders.

5 Add the butter bits, baking powder, and salt while you quickly stir the mixture.

6 When the butter is completely absorbed, mix in the eggs.

7 Pour the mixture into the baking dish. Bake for 40 minutes.

8 When the spoon bread has cooled a bit, but is still warm, serve it up!

A Western Life Board Game

The activities in this book have helped you learn about life in the West. The people who settled there after 1862 worked hard. They raised crops, built ranches, and established new businesses and cities. Many succeeded, some suffered through bad times, and some failed.

Most settlers never saw a Native American. Yet the settlers changed the lives of Native Americans forever. When you design and make your board game, use everything you've learned about settling the West. Then share what you know when you play your game with your family and friends.

a game board from
"The Game of Cats and Mice," 1885

Design a New Board Game

YOUR GOAL:

Design, construct, and then play a board game about life in the West.

WHAT YOU'LL NEED:

- the research materials you've used for the other activities in this book
- 15 inch x 15 inch square of heavy cardboard
- paints and brushes, colored markers, colored pencils, and/or crayons
- a pencil
- one dark-colored marker
- ruler
- paper
- a die
- buttons, coins, or other small objects to use as markers

TIME NEEDED:

2–3 hours

What to Do:

RESEARCH THE SUBJECT

1 Review all the research materials you have gathered and made about life in the West.

2 Make a list of seven events that you would enjoy if you were a settler in the West. Here's an example: Went to a Fourth of July picnic.

3 Now list seven unpleasant events. Here's an example: Wagon wheel got stuck in mud.

DESIGN THE GAME BOARD

1 Using the ruler and pencil, draw a border of 3-inch squares along the edges of the cardboard. When you're done, there will be one square in each corner and three squares between them (16 squares in all). When you're sure the squares are done correctly, go over your pencil lines with the dark marker.

Using the dark marker, label the square in the lower left corner of the board "Start." This is where the game will begin.

Label the square just to the right of the starting square "Bonanza!" This is where the game will end.

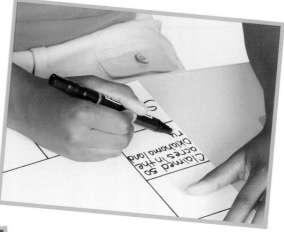

In each of the remaining squares, write one of the 14 events on your list. Be sure to alternate pleasant and unpleasant events, for variety during playing.

5 Under each pleasant event write, "Jump ahead 1 square," "Jump ahead 2 squares," or "Jump ahead 3 squares."

6 Under each unpleasant event write, "Move back 1 square," "Move back 2 squares," or "Move back 3 squares."

7 Decorate your game board. Using markers, paints, or colored pencils, color the squares. Draw any kind of western scene that you like in the center of the board.

PLAY THE GAME

1 Each player chooses a marker and places it on the "Start" square.

2 The players take turns throwing the die.

3 Each player moves her or his marker clockwise the number of squares shown on the die.

4 The player reads the directions on the square and moves forward or back according to the directions.

5 The winner is the first player to land on or pass the "Bonanza!" square.

Glossary

blacksmith	(BLAK-smihth) a person who works with iron, melting and shaping it (page 6)
chorus	(KOR-uhs) a part of a song that is repeated (page 16)
column	(KAHL-uhm) a row of words running down a page (page 9)
draft	(DRAFT) the first, rough version of a piece of writing (page 9)
headline	(HEHD-lighn) the title of a newspaper article (page 8)
ingredient	(ihn-GREE-dee-ehnt) a food item in a recipe (page 20)
layout	(LAY-owt) a planned arrangement of items (page 10)
pioneer	(pigh-uh-NEER) a person who is one of the first to do something or go somewhere (page 2)
proofread	(PROOF-reed) to read carefully to find errors in spelling, punctuation, or grammar (page 9)
prospector	(PRAH-spehk-ter) a person who looks for gold (page 2)
reservation	(rehz-er-VAY-shuhn) an area of land set aside for Native Americans to live on (page 4)
revise	(ree-VIHZ) to make changes to a piece of writing (page 9)
settle	(SEHT-uhl) to set up a home in a new place (page 2)
transcontinental	(tranz-kahn-tih-NEHNT-uhl) something that goes from one end of a continent to the other (page 3)
verse	(VERS) a section of a song or poem that usually rhymes (page 16)

Index